T0164185

The Effect of Reserve Activations and Active-Duty Deployments on Local Employment During the Global War on Terrorism

David S. Loughran, Jacob Alex Klerman,
Bogdan Savych

The research descibed in this report results from the RAND Corporation's continuing program of self-initiated independent research. Support for such research is provided, in part, by donors and by the independent research and development provisions of RAND's contracts for the operation of its U.S. Department of Defense federally funded research and development centers.

Library of Congress Cataloging-in-Publication Data is available for this publication.

ISBN 0-8330-3900-8

The RAND Corporation is a nonprofit research organization providing objective analysis and effective solutions that address the challenges facing the public and private sectors around the world. RAND's publications do not necessarily reflect the opinions of its research clients and sponsors.

RAND® is a registered trademark.

Published 2006 by the RAND Corporation
1776 Main Street, P.O. Box 2138, Santa Monica, CA 90407-2138
1200 South Hayes Street, Arlington, VA 22202-5050
201 North Craig Street, Suite 202, Pittsburgh, PA 15213-1516
RAND URL: http://www.rand.org/
To order RAND documents or to obtain additional information, contact
Distribution Services: Telephone: (310) 451-7002;
Fax: (310) 451-6915; Email: order@rand.org

PREFACE

This report presents an econometric analysis of the impact of active-duty and reserve activations and deployments on local economic conditions as measured by changes in local employment. The project is part of a broader research agenda at the RAND Corporation studying how activations and deployments impact the lives of reservists, their families, and their communities. The results of this study will be of particular interest to policymakers, researchers, and other individuals interested in the impact of activations and deployments on local economic conditions.

This report results from RAND's continuing program of self-initiated independent research. Support for such research is provided, in part, by donors and by the independent research and development provisions of RAND's contracts for the operation of its U.S. Department of Defense federally funded research and development centers.

This research was conducted within the RAND National Security Research Division (NSRD). NSRD conducts research and analysis for the Office of the Secretary of Defense, the Joint Staff, the Unified Commands, the defense agencies, the Department of the Navy, the U.S. Intelligence Community, allied foreign governments, and foundations.

For more information on the RAND National Security Research Division, contact the Director of Operations, Nurith Berstein. She can be reached by email at nurith_berstein@rand.org; by phone at 703-413-1100, extension 5469; or by mail at RAND Corporation, 1200 South Hayes Street, Arlington, VA 22202-5050. More information about RAND is available at www.rand.org.

CONTENTS

FIGURES

TABLES

SUMMARY

The ongoing Global War on Terrorism has resulted in the largest deployment of American service personnel since the Vietnam War. Large numbers of active-duty forces have been deployed overseas; large numbers of reservists have been activated and deployed overseas as well. These activations and deployments have stimulated concerns about their effect on the local economies in which active-duty forces are stationed and in which reservists live in peacetime.

This report presents an econometric analysis of the impact of activations and deployments on local economic conditions as measured by changes in local employment. We begin by noting that the overall effect of activations and deployments on total U.S. employment cannot be large. The U.S. economy employs about 126 million workers. The number of reservists activated or deployed from U.S. counties for Global War on Terrorism contingencies in a given month peaked in 2003 at about 160,000, which represents roughly 0.13 percent of the U.S. workforce. If we add in deployed active-duty personnel at their monthly peak in 2003 (about 140,000), activated and deployed personnel represented, at most, 0.20 percent of the U.S. workforce during our study period (2001–2004).

However, active-duty forces are concentrated on a relatively small number of military bases, and reserve units, by nature, are geographically concentrated. Thus, even though the national effect of deployment and activation is likely to be small, it is possible that the effect on some firms and communities is much larger. Some employers might have trouble replacing activated reserve personnel in the short run, leading to declines in output and profitability. And, in some communities, the absence of activated reserve and deployed active-duty personnel could depress local demand for goods and services.

Despite these concerns, there has been little systematic analysis of the impact of reserve activations and active-duty deployments on local economic conditions. To address this gap in our understanding of the issue, we estimate econometric models to measure the impact of activations and deployments on local employment. We measure employment at the county level as recorded by the Bureau of Labor Statistics and generate counts of activated and deployed reserve and active-duty personnel from the Defense Manpower Data Center Global War on Terrorism Contingency File.

FINDINGS

For reserve activations, our estimates imply a nearly one-for-one decline in employment with activation in the short run. However, four months after activation, employment has returned to its pre-activation level. From these results, we infer that employers can and do hire replacement workers for activated reserve personnel and that this process requires several months to complete.

For active-duty deployments, our estimates imply an increase of about one civilian employee for every ten deploying active-duty service members. We suggest two possible explanations for this finding. One possibility is that base commanders hire civilians to backfill for some tasks previously performed by deploying active-duty service members (e.g., security, grounds maintenance). A second possibility is that the spouses of active-duty personnel enter the civilian labor market when their husbands or wives are deployed. In either case, active-duty deployments could generate a small increase in local employment while those active-duty personnel are deployed.

We acknowledge that other interpretations of these empirical findings are possible. Our econometric model estimates the correlation between equilibrium employment and activations and deployments, and so it cannot distinguish between supply- and demand-side explanations of why employment might respond to activations and deployments. For reasons discussed in the main body of the report, we prefer the supply-side interpretation of the results given above, but it is possible that activations and deployments affect local demand, which in turn affects the demand for labor. In the case of reserve activations, for example, it is possible that employment declines in the short run because local demand for goods and services falls when reservists depart for active-duty service.

We infer from our empirical findings that reserve activations and active-duty deployments of the magnitude experienced during the Global War on Terrorism are not likely to have significant long-term impacts on local economic conditions, at least as measured by aggregate employment. However, we do acknowledge that some specific communities and some specific employers could suffer when their reserve employees are activated. For example, we provide suggestive evidence that police departments might find it particularly difficult to replace activated reservists in the short run and that this could be particularly true in smaller communities. The Department of Defense's policy of exempting reservists from active-duty service whose absence could adversely affect national security (broadly construed) is sensitive to this concern. Further research is needed to understand how other economic indicators (e.g., revenues, profits) respond to the loss of activated reserve personnel.

FUTURE RESEARCH

Future research might pay special attention to the impact of activations on smaller firms and the self-employed, neither of which could be examined specifically with these data. The self-employed might be examined most fruitfully at the individual level, since individual earnings are most likely to be the best barometer of their financial well-being. Although the following claim needs to be empirically validated, we note that standard economic principles would argue against finding substantial negative impacts of activations on the income of self-employed reservists. These self-employed reservists presumably chose reserve service because they thought it would, on net, benefit them. Consequently, we would not expect individuals who stand to lose their businesses if called to active duty to put themselves at risk of activation, unless these individuals uniformly have unusually strong preferences for military service and unusually weak preferences for their civilian work. In ongoing work, we find that the self-employed, on average, experience large earnings gains when activated; what happens to their earnings when they return from active duty is unknown at this time.

Similar reasoning might also apply to very small firms. While overt discrimination against reservists in hiring decisions is illegal, it seems entirely possible that employers could know whether a given applicant is a member of the Reserves and find legitimate reasons not to hire that individual if it seems too risky to do so. That is, we would not expect small employers to take large risks in hiring reservists who might one day be activated if those employers are not compelled or do not find it optimal to do so.

ACKNOWLEDGMENTS

This technical report details results from the RAND Independent Research and Development (IR&D) program project "The Impact of Reserve Activations on Employers." The project builds on insights and database preparation conducted as part of the RAND project "The Effect of Activation on the Earnings of Reservists," sponsored by the Office of the Secretary of Defense—Reserve Affairs (OSD-RA). That project's databases were constructed with the support and cooperation of staff in the Defense Manpower Data Center (DMDC) and OSD-RA. Scott Seggerman and Barbara Balison at DMDC patiently answered our questions and promptly transferred data to us. At OSD-RA, John Winkler, Michael Price, Richard Krimmer, Virginia Highland, and Tom Bush helped with our data requests and in understanding DMDC databases; they also offered valuable comments and suggestions on the content of the study as it progressed.

We have benefited from the support and guidance of the former and current Directors of RAND's Forces and Resources Policy Program in the National Defense Research Institute: Susan Everingham and James Hosek, respectively. We also benefited from the careful reviews of this report provided by Glenn Gotz of the Institute for Defense Analyses and John Romley of RAND. Also at RAND, Craig Martin provided outstanding programming support, Christopher Dirks and Natasha Kostan helped with the preparation of the manuscript, and Paul Steinberg provided editorial support.

Finally, we acknowledge the financial support and guidance of RAND's IR&D program.

ACRONYMS

BLS	Bureau of Labor Statistics
CBO	Congressional Budget Office
DMDC	Defense Manpower Data Center
DoD	Department of Defense
EMT	emergency medical technician
MP	military police
NAICS	North American Industry Classification System
OCONUS	outside the continental United States
OSD-RA	Office of the Secretary of Defense—Reserve Affairs
PUMA	Public Use Microdata Area
QCEW	Quarterly Census of Employment and Wages
SESA	State Employment Security Agencies
SOFRC	Status of Forces Survey of Reserve Component Members
SWA	Southwest Asia
USERRA	Uniformed Services Employment and Reemployment Rights Act

1. INTRODUCTION

BACKGROUND

The ongoing Global War on Terrorism represents the largest deployment of American military power since the Vietnam War. The Global War on Terrorism has sustained high-tempo military operations for more than three years, and the Department of Defense (DoD) projects that operations in support of the Global War on Terrorism will continue for at least several more years. Hundreds of thousands of active-duty soldiers have been deployed from bases within the continental United States, and hundreds of thousands of reservists have been called to active duty and deployed overseas. These recent events have raised concern within DoD, within the reserve and active-duty communities, and among policymakers that large-scale and sustained activations and deployments might adversely affect service members, their families, and their communities in a variety of ways. This report examines the impact of activations and deployments on local employment.[1]

Local employment could be negatively affected by activations and deployments for two reasons. First, the Uniformed Services Employment and Reemployment Rights Act (USERRA) guarantees activated reservists the right to return to their pre-activation job following activation, providing the job still exists. Therefore, employers of reservists cannot permanently replace activated reservists with new hires. Instead, they must find internal or temporary replacements for these workers. Alternatively, employers could leave the positions unfilled, which could make it difficult for them to maintain their pre-activation level of productivity.

Second, the demand for local goods might decline when reservists and active-duty members leave their communities, for two reasons. First, the reservists and active duty-members themselves are no longer present

---

[1] We also examined the impact of activations and deployments on local earnings (wages and salary). These analyses, described in Appendix A, produced anomalous results, which we attribute to data-related problems.

to demand goods and services from local businesses; second, the families of these service members might temporarily leave the community as well, further depressing demand.

Despite these concerns, there has been little systematic analysis of the impact of reserve activations and active-duty deployments on local economic conditions. Separate stories in the *Washington Post* (Finer, 2005) and the *Los Angeles Times* (Mehren, 2005) described the impact of reserve activations on local communities in Vermont, a state with an unusually high proportion of its population serving on active duty as reservists. One story describes the effect of having 88 men deployed from the rural town of Enosburg Falls, which, at the time the article was written, had a population of only 1,437; those 88 men are likely to represent about a quarter of prime-age males. The workers remaining are described as working long hours and covering multiple jobs (Mehren, 2005). According to the *Washington Post*'s story, the loss of police and fire personnel have meant that some local public safety jobs are not being performed at their previous level (Finer, 2005).[2]

Both stories quoted the same plant manager at a local seed company on how activations have affected his firm:

> We've been hit hard. Some of these are highly specialized jobs, so it is very hard to find people who can step in and replace them [activated reserves]. And no one wants to come from another company when they know that these guys will come back in a year and a half. (Finer, 2005)

and

> Everyone is working extra hard, and we have gone to a temp agency to try to fill the vacancies. It affects us because we have lost people with years of experience. You can't replace that. We have lost skill, not just employees. (Mehren, 2005)

---

[2] An additional story on reserve activations from Johnstown, Pennsylvania, notes that 21 employees of the Somerset correctional facility, including 18 guards, are serving on active duty, forcing some overtime work among the remaining guards and the hiring of some interim employees (Infield, 2005).

We are aware of two published studies that have employed administrative or survey data to analyze how reserve activations affect local economic conditions. The Congressional Budget Office (CBO) (2005) combined descriptive data on reservists and their employers with data from 19 interviews with employers of reservists (including the self-employed) to draw conclusions about the potential effect of activation on employers. CBO notes, as we do below, that the scope of the problem is likely to be small because, by its estimates, only 6 percent of all business establishments employ reservists. Nonetheless, CBO argues that smaller firms, the self-employed, and firms employing reservists with highly specialized skills might be vulnerable to negative economic impacts attributable to activations. Combining data from the Defense Manpower Data Center (DMDC) on the characteristics of firms that employ reservists and the occupations of reservists within those firms, CBO (2005) estimates that about 0.6 percent of small businesses and 0.5 percent of self-employed individuals could be affected by the loss of a crucial employee (or owner) to activation.

Doyle et al. (2004) echo this concern in their report based on interviews with eight small businesses that received Military Reservist Economic Impact Disaster Loans. These loans are intended to help small businesses that have been adversely affected by the loss of activated reserve personnel. These interviewed firms reported losing business while their reserve employees were activated and even after they returned to work. The select nature of their sample, though, prevents them from generalizing their results to small businesses in general.

In addition to the impact on local businesses, public officials have expressed concern that reserve activations could adversely affect public safety employers. Unpublished analyses of the November 2004 Status of Forces Survey of Reserve Component Members (SOFRC) by DMDC (2005) show that about 17 percent of reserve respondents work as first responders and 18 percent work in emergency services.[3] Of these

---

[3] Respondents could hold multiple jobs or work in multiple capacities in the same job, causing the sum of these percentages to exceed 100. The survey defines first responders as "[m]en and women who are first on the scene as a domestic disaster (natural or man-made) unfolds. First responders are generally state or local law enforcement officers (including SWAT teams, bomb-dog teams, and bomb squads),

reservists working as first responders, 53 percent reported working full time, 18 percent reported working part time, and 35 percent reported working as volunteers. Comparable percentages of reservists reported working as emergency responders. These statistics make clear that reservists are much more likely to work in public safety occupations than are non-reservists. In the 2000 U.S. Census, for example, only about 6 percent of males aged 18 to 40 reported working in public safety occupations. Unfortunately, it is difficult to extrapolate reliably from these statistics to infer how many public safety employers are potentially affected by reserve activations.

OBJECTIVES AND LIMITATIONS

In this report, we seek to analyze systematically how local economies respond to activations and deployments. We do so by employing econometric panel-data methods to analyze how variation in monthly counts of activated reserve and deployed active-duty military personnel correlates with variation in monthly employment at the county level.[4] Our data permit us to disaggregate our results by county size and, to a very limited extent, by employer type. More disaggregated analyses might become more feasible in the future with the completion of DMDC's Civilian Employer Information database, which records detailed information from Dun & Bradstreet on most employers of currently employed selected reservists. Nonetheless, the results we report here provide a first systematic look at how local employment responds to activations and deployments in the short run.

Our focus is on the short-run impact of activations and deployments. More research is needed to understand the long-run impact

---

firefighters (including Hazardous Material and Search and Rescue personnel), and Emergency Medical Technicians." Emergency services refers to "[m]embers of federal, state, or local organizations (agencies and private) such as: emergency communication centers, hospital emergency trauma centers, state and local public health, emergency/disaster management, transportation and public works, public utilities (water, gas, electric, telephone, etc.) emergency repair personnel, Federal Search and Rescue personnel, law enforcement, HAZMAT, medical trauma teams, and some members of the American Red Cross."

[4] Our econometric analyses are similar in spirit to those employed to study the impact of base closure and realignment on local economic conditions during the 1990s (e.g., Hooker and Knetter, 1999; Poppert and Herzog, 2003).

of activations and deployments on profits and whether activations and deployments are particularly burdensome to smaller businesses and communities. We also note here that this report does not fully address the important question of how reserve activations affect the provision of local public safety and homeland defense (e.g., firefighters, police officers, emergency medical technicians [EMTs], National Guard members, and other "first responders"). Reservists are much more likely than other individuals to be employed in public safety occupations and, obviously, in the National Guard, and it could be particularly difficult for public safety employers to replace activated reservists in the short run. The appropriate balance between domestic and foreign uses of the National Guard is also at issue.[5]

DEFINITIONS

Before proceeding, we need to define what we mean when we say "activated" or "activation" versus "deployed" or "deployment." For data-related reasons (see Section 3), we use the term "activated" throughout this document to refer generically to a state of serving on active duty as a reservist in support of the Global War on Terrorism and its specific contingencies (i.e., Operation Noble Eagle, Operation Enduring Freedom, and Operation Iraqi Freedom). An "activated" reservist may or may not be "deployed." For the purposes of this report, being "deployed" means serving outside the continental United States (OCONUS) in support of a Global War on Terrorism contingency. In most cases, "deployed" also means serving in an officially designated combat zone. Thus, in the context of the Global War on Terrorism, a reservist whose home base is in California and who is backfilling a military position in Georgia would be considered "activated" but not "deployed." For this report, we analyze the impact of reserve activations, regardless of whether activated reservists were deployed, since being activated means, in all likelihood, suspending work for a civilian employer. For regular active-duty personnel, being "deployed" means leaving one's active-duty base for military operations in a combat zone.

---

[5] See, for example, Brown et al. (1997).

Finally, throughout this report, when we refer to the Reserves, we mean the Selected Reserve and the Individual Ready Reserve, which include both the Reserves and National Guard and the separate components within them (Army Reserve, Army National Guard, Air Force Reserve, Air National Guard, Navy Reserve, Marine Corps Reserve, and the Coast Guard Reserve) but exclude the Standby Reserve, Retired Reserve, and Inactive National Guard. Direct mobilizations from the Individual Ready Reserve have been relatively rare during the Global War on Terrorism, but these individuals are included in our data.

ORGANIZATION OF THIS REPORT

This report proceeds in five sections. The next section places our specific research questions in the broader context of the Global War on Terrorism and discusses why activations and deployments could have a negative impact on employment. Section 3 then describes our data and the methods we employ to analyze them. In Section 4, we present estimates derived from our econometric model of employment. We conclude in Section 5 with our findings and their implications for military manpower policy.

2. THE POLICY CONTEXT

In this section, we first provide descriptive statistics on the absolute magnitude of reserve activations and active-duty deployments during the Global War on Terrorism and their magnitude relative to total U.S. employment. We then consider the possible ways that activation and deployment might affect local employment.

ACTIVATIONS AND DEPLOYMENTS DURING THE GLOBAL WAR ON TERRORISM

By historical standards, the use of reserve forces since September 11, 2001, has been extraordinary (see Figure 2.1). During fiscal year 2004, reservists contributed approximately 63 million duty days in support of the Global War on Terrorism, which is five times the duty days provided in fiscal year 2000 and half again as large as the duty days provided during Operations Desert Shield/Desert Storm.

The duration of the average reserve activation has also been long by historical standards. Between September 2001 and December 2004, the average activation lasted eight months; moreover, this duration underestimates the true length of activations, since many activation spells had yet to be completed. About 21 percent of activated reservists (some 73,000 reservists) had been activated more than once since September 11, 2001.

As the figure shows, even before September 11, 2001, reserve activations were increasing steadily because DoD was increasingly relying on reserve forces for small-scale military operations and peacekeeping operations (e.g., operations in Haiti, Bosnia, Southwest Asia [SWA], and Kosovo). Still, all the evidence suggests that the events of September 11 and the subsequent scale of reserve mobilizations were unexpected. Thus, it is reasonable to assume that prior to September 11, employers and local communities did not expect their reserve members to be activated and deployed to the extent they have been. As we discuss later in this section and in Section 3, this assumption is important in interpreting the results of our econometric model.

Figure 2.1
Active-Duty Days Contributed by the Reserve Components,
by Fiscal Year

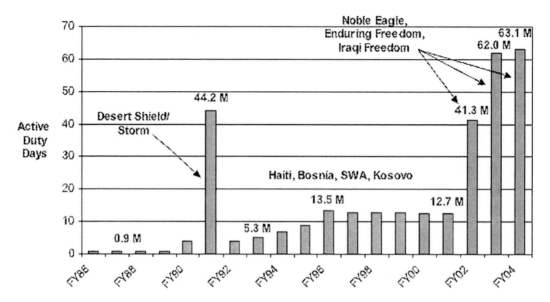

SOURCE: Reproduced from unpublished figures created by the Office of
the Secretary of Defense—Reserve Affairs (OSD-RA).

Figure 2.2 shows the mean monthly number of active-duty and reserve
personnel living in U.S. counties activated or deployed in support of
the Global War on Terrorism between September 2001 and December 2004.[6]
The figure shows that the mean number of reserve personnel activated in
support of Global War on Terrorism contingencies was moderate in 2001
and 2002 (33,000 and 62,000, respectively), reflecting the more limited
use of the Reserves in Afghanistan and domestically for homeland
defense. However, the mean number of reserve personnel activated
increased sharply in 2003 and 2004 with Operation Iraqi Freedom and the
subsequent, ongoing reconstruction and peacekeeping efforts in Iraq. The

---

[6] Figure 2.2 counts only personnel activated or deployed from U.S. counties and
so undercounts total activations and deployments in support of the Global War on
Terrorism. Reserve activations and deployment are undercounted by approximately 2
percent. Active-duty deployments are undercounted by 36 percent. Many active-duty
troops are deployed from OCONUS locations. Also, active-duty personnel whose duty
location is a ship are not included in these counts. For reasons explained in Section
3, these figures may still undercount the actual number of active-duty personnel
deployed from U.S. counties.

figure also shows the mean number of reserve personnel deployed in support of the Global War on Terrorism, which displays a similar time trend but is small relative to the number of activated personnel. The reserve forces are instrumental in operating and maintaining ongoing military operations, and many of those required functions (e.g., training, administrative processing, operating mobilization and demobilization facilities, staffing medical facilities, maintaining equipment, intelligence) are performed domestically. Additionally, reservists who deploy can spend several months training to deploy and undergoing demobilization exercises following deployment, and some reservists backfill for active-duty personnel deployed from domestic bases.

Figure 2.2
Mean Number of Military Personnel Activated and Deployed per Month, by Year (000)

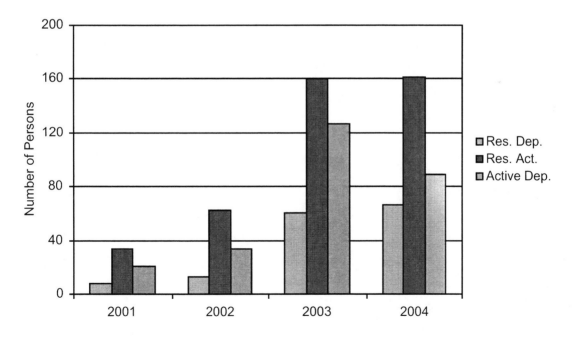

SOURCE: Global War on Terrorism Contingency File.
NOTE: Figures count activations and deployments originating in U.S. counties.

These aggregate figures on reserve activations suggest that the impact of activations on aggregate U.S. employment is likely to be very small. Over the time period covered by Figure 2.2, the U.S economy employed an average of 126 million persons in any given month. Thus, on average, activated reservists have represented a tiny percentage—between 0.03 percent in 2001 and 0.13 percent in 2004—of total U.S employment during the Global War on Terrorism. Moreover, not all activated reservists are employed in civilian occupations prior to being activated, and so each activated reservist does not necessarily represent an individual who would otherwise be employed in a civilian job.

However, reservists are not distributed proportionally to populations across the United States. Table 2.1 shows the distribution of the ratio of activated reservists to total employment at the county level between September 2001 and December 2004. The ratio of reserve activations to total employment varies by nearly an order of magnitude between the 25th and 75th percentiles of the overall distribution, although the overall magnitude of the ratio is generally quite small.

Reserve activations equal or exceed 1 percent of county employment in only slightly more than 1 percent of all county-month observations. As Table 2.1 shows, these counties are considerably smaller than other counties.[7] In fact, employment declines steadily as reserve activations as a fraction of employment increase (with the exception of counties with no reserve activations). Counties with activations totaling at least 1 percent of employment have an average employment of 3,655. This compares with median county employment of 8,147 and mean employment of 56,617 at the median value of the ratio of reserve activations to employment. Counties in which reserve activations constitute at least 1 percent of employment tend to persist in that state as well. Over the span of our data, these counties spent an average of 12 months in which reserve activations constituted at least 1 percent of employment.

---

[7] This result is not unexpected. If all reserve units were the same size, then we would expect a larger percentage of a county's employment to be activated in smaller counties. The result is not exact. Reserve units vary in size. Sometimes multiple units are activated from the same county (but usually only for larger counties).

Table 2.1
County Employment by Ratio of Reserve Activations to Employment

County Percentile Arrayed by Reserve Activations/Employment	Reserve Activations/ Employment	County Employment
13	0	11,095
20	0.0002	85,825
25	0.0003	56,996
50	0.0009	56,617
75	0.002	28,740
80	0.002	20,194
95	0.006	10,780
98	0.009	5,921
99	0.014	3,720

While large numbers of active-duty personnel have been deployed from domestic bases during the Global War on Terrorism (see Figure 2.2), these deployments have originated in a comparatively small number of counties. While more than 98 percent of all U.S. counties had at least one resident reservist serve on active duty over the span of our data, only 14 percent of all counties experienced the deployment of active-duty personnel. These counties tend to be quite large. Counties that deployed any active-duty personnel during the span of our data have a median employment of 84,028, compared with a median employment of 8,464 in counties with activated reservists.

HOW ACTIVATION AND DEPLOYMENT MIGHT AFFECT LOCAL EMPLOYMENT: A MODEL

Activations and deployments could affect local economic conditions in a variety of ways. Largely for reasons related to data availability, we choose in this report to measure those economic impacts via employment.[8] Thus, our key research question is: How does activation and deployment affect local civilian employment? Here, we present a simple model that helps us to discuss that question more formally.

Consider the following model of total employment, N, in geographic area g and period t:

$$N_{gt} = \mu_g + R_{gt}\beta + A_{gt}\gamma + X_{gt}\theta, \qquad (2.1)$$

---

[8] See Appendix A for results related to local earnings (wages and salary).

where μ represents baseline employment, R is the number of reservists activated, A is the number of active-duty personnel deployed, and X captures other determinants of employment. In this section, we use this model to discuss why reserve activations and active-duty deployments might affect local employment, deferring discussion of how we estimate this model econometrically to the next section.

We divide our discussion into "supply-side" and "demand-side" hypotheses. By "supply-side" hypotheses, we mean hypotheses related to the supply of labor to employers; by "demand-side" hypotheses, we mean hypotheses related to the demand for labor by employers.

Supply-Side Hypotheses

We begin by considering supply-side hypotheses. One possibility is that civilian and military employers do not find replacement workers for activated reservists or deployed active-duty personnel. Assuming all activated reservists hold civilian jobs prior to their activation, this hypothesis implies $\beta = -1$. That is, every reservist leaves a civilian job when activated, and that reservist is not subsequently replaced. Since active-duty personnel are not counted in our measure of employment (see Section 3), this same hypothesis implies that active-duty deployments have no effect on civilian employment ($\gamma = 0$).

An alternative supply-side hypothesis posits that civilian and military employers replace workers lost to activation or deployment instantaneously. Under this hypothesis, reserve activations have no impact on civilian employment ($\beta = 0$). Active-duty deployments, on the other hand, increase civilian employment one-for-one ($\gamma = 1$) if military bases replace (i.e., backfill) deployed active-duty personnel with civilian workers (e.g., private security officers, civilian maintenance workers).

In general, we might expect the truth to lie somewhere between these two polar supply-side hypotheses. Consider reserve activations. Most obviously, not all activated reservists are employed in the civilian sector prior to activation. Some reservists are full-time students; others might be looking for work; and still others might be retired or work at home. If this is true, then employment will decline by less than the number of activated reservists.

In addition, we might expect civilian employers to replace some, but not necessarily all, of their reserve employees who leave for active duty. Two factors affect the ability of civilian employers to replace activated reservists. First, the ability of employers to replace activated reservists with temporary workers might be limited by tight local labor markets and scarcity of workers with specific skills. Second, USERRA grants reservists the right to be reemployed by their pre-activation employer. Consequently, employers will generally want to hire replacement workers with the understanding that their employment is temporary. The short-term nature of such employment will diminish the attractiveness of training a new, but temporary, employee (CBO, 2005). Comparably skilled temporary workers could demand higher wages to account for lower job security, or, conversely, the firm might settle for a less-skilled worker at the same wage. However, if job turnover in the economy is sufficiently high, then hiring temporary workers might not be a significant problem. This consideration would also cause employment to decline by less than the number of reserve activations.

Now consider the reasons active-duty deployments might not affect employment according to either of the two polar supply-side hypotheses discussed above. First, some active-duty soldiers also work civilian jobs (i.e., moonlight during off-duty hours). Civilian employment would, therefore, decline when these active-duty soldiers are deployed. Second, military bases are unlikely to backfill all of the active-duty positions with temporary civilian replacements. Presumably, a relatively small number of jobs on a military base is essential for that base to continue functioning during a period of large-scale deployments.

Demand-Side Hypotheses

Demand-side hypotheses posit that the departure of reservists and active-duty personnel from local communities depresses demand for local goods and services and, therefore, decreases the demand for labor. Most directly, activated and deployed reserve personnel are no longer present to consume local goods and services. Declines in the supply of or demand for labor could also occur if spouses of reservists and active-duty personnel leave their jobs when their husband or wife departs on active duty or even leave the local area to move in with family members in other locations (e.g., to get help with child care).

Alternatively, activations and deployments could actually increase the demand for local goods and services. For example, with the service member away, family demand for local services (e.g., restaurant meals, child care, home repair services, car repair) might increase. The income of reservists and active-duty personnel tends to increase while serving on active duty or when deployed OCONUS (see Klerman, Loughran, and Martin, 2005), thus providing income with which to fund the higher family demand for local goods and services.

Ultimately, we estimate reduced-form regressions of equilibrium employment on activations and deployments that cannot, strictly speaking, distinguish between these various supply- and demand-side hypotheses. For example, if we find that employment falls as reserve activations increase, we cannot say with certainty that this is because local labor markets made it prohibitively expensive for employers to replace these activated reservists. It could be that employment fell because the local demand for goods and services, and hence labor, fell as a result of the activations. As we argue in Section 4, we find the supply-side explanations to be more plausible, but admit that we cannot rule out demand-side explanations, too.

IMPACT ON SMALL FIRMS AND PUBLIC SAFETY EMPLOYERS

The preceding discussion focused on average effects, but it is likely that some firms will have more trouble than others adjusting to the temporary absence of their reserve employees. Smaller firms have been a source of particular concern and the target of specific policy actions. Our tabulations of the May 2004 SOFRC imply that about 24 percent of employed reservists work for firms with fewer than 100 employees and that about 6 percent are self-employed.[9] About 10 percent

---

[9] Authors' computations based on extract of May 2004 SOFRC. The percentage of reservists working for firms with fewer than 100 employees (24 percent) is considerably larger than what was reported by reservists surveyed in the 2000 Reserve Component Survey (18 percent). The May 2004 SOFRC has a low response rate (about 37

of reservists work for firms with fewer than 10 employees, and 15 percent work for firms with fewer than 25 employees.

Smaller firms may be less able to accommodate temporarily the loss of a key employee by reallocating their current workforce and may be more vulnerable to hiring and training costs associated with replacing an activated reservist in the short run. Recognizing this potential problem, the Small Business Administration offers special loans to small businesses that can demonstrate that the loss of an activated reservist has had a negative impact on the firm's finances. The loans can total up to $1.5 million, are available at an interest rate of 4 percent or less, and have a maximum term of 30 years. According to CBO (2005), under this program the Small Business Administration has awarded more than 200 loans totaling $18 million since 2001.

Another focus of attention has been on public safety employers, who employ large numbers of reservists. For example, in a September 2004 speech, Senator Hillary Rodham Clinton (D-N.Y.) stated:

> While we need to be thinking of ways in which the National Guard can contribute to homeland security, we need to be sure that the pattern of Guard and reserve deployments do not actually end up hindering homeland security. In many communities throughout our nation, a significant number of police officers, firefighters, and EMTs, who are first responders in case of attack, are also members of the Guard or reserves. And in a time of large-scale activations and extended deployments, many communities are being left short handed without enough police, firefighters and EMTs to handle a major crisis. (Clinton, 2004)

The loss of public safety employees (e.g., police officers, firefighters, EMTs, public health officials) to activation is probably felt most acutely in small communities that employ small numbers of these personnel and may not have ready access to trained replacements. By law, DoD can grant waivers or delay activation for reservists whose activation would result in severe personal hardship or in hardship for their community, or that would seriously harm their employer's ability

---

percent), so its results may not generalize accurately to the entire reserve population. See DMDC (2004) for more on the administration and content of the SOFRC.

to perform functions essential to the nation's defense, health, or safety. Between September 2001 and August 2005, DoD granted 144 waivers and 116 delays to reservists, a very large proportion of which were for federal employees or state and local first responders.

3. DATA AND METHODS

We describe our data and methods in this section, first explaining how we measure employment and then how to measure activations and deployments. We then explain our econometric methods and detail the specific hypotheses these methods allow us to test.

MEASURING LOCAL EMPLOYMENT

We draw information on local employment from the Quarterly Census of Employment and Wages (QCEW).[10] All employers whose workers are covered by state and federal unemployment insurance programs are required to pay quarterly unemployment insurance taxes on wages. Using these quarterly reports to State Employment Security Agencies (SESAs), the Bureau of Labor Statistics (BLS) generates aggregate statistics on employment by economic sector and geographic area (state, consolidated metropolitan statistical area, metropolitan statistical area, and county). We employ monthly and quarterly data from these aggregate reports between January 2001 and December 2004.[11]

In 2004, approximately 8.5 million establishments provided information to SESAs. These establishments employ virtually all nonagricultural employees and about 47 percent of workers employed in agricultural industries (BLS, 2005). Major exclusions from these data are self-employed workers, religious organizations, most agricultural workers on small farms, active-duty military personnel, elected officials in most states, most employees of railroads, some domestic workers, unpaid family workers, most student workers attending school, and certain employees of small nonprofit organizations.

In the aggregate data, employment is recorded monthly. Employment is defined as the number of individuals who received wages or salary

---

[10] The data are available online at ftp://ftp.bls.gov/pub/special.requests/cew/ (as of November 2005). Our version of the data is current as of September 13, 2005.

[11] In 2001, the QCEW began collecting and reporting data based on the North American Industry Classification System (NAICS) rather than the Standard Industrial Classification (SIC) system. This change in reporting causes some issues of data comparability before 2001. We begin our analysis in January 2001; thus, our results are not affected by this reporting problem.

during the pay period that includes the 12th day of the month. As explained in BLS (1997), the employment measure includes all corporation officials, executives, supervisory personnel, clerical workers, wage earners, pieceworkers, and part-time workers. Workers are reported in the state and county of the physical location of their job. This measure of employment includes all workers on paid sick leave, holiday, and vacation, but excludes those on leave without pay for the entire payroll period.

This definition of employment is problematic for our analyses in cases in which activated reservists continue to receive wages from their civilian employer, either because the employer is willing to pay reservists part or all of their salary, even though they are absent from work, or because reservists use vacation and other paid leave when serving on active duty. The receipt of paid leave will confound our analyses in the very short run if reservists do in fact take paid leave when activated. The receipt of wages throughout the period of activation is even more problematic. About 16 percent of activated reservists who responded to the May 2004 SOFRC claimed that their civilian employers continued to pay them part or all of their salary for their entire period of activation. Another 16 percent reported that they received civilian compensation for part of the period of activation. However, because of a low survey response rate (about 37 percent of eligible respondents), we do not know whether that estimate generalizes to the entire population of activated reservists.[12] In as much as activated reservists only receive benefits (e.g., health insurance, pension), BLS instructions imply that they should not be counted as employed.

Nominally, the QCEW data include information on monthly employment by county (the finest level of geographic detail)[13] and by detailed NAICS industry. In practice, confidentiality concerns lead to the suppression of much of the information at the county-industry level. Consequently, we cannot implement industry-specific regressions at the

---

[12] See DMDC (2004).

[13] The borders of two counties and their neighboring counties changed slightly during our sample period. We made minor adjustments to our employment counts to account for this change in borders. Details are available from the authors upon request.

county level. We do, however, report results of regressions on public safety employment at the state level implemented for the 34 states that disclosed public safety employment in our data.

MEASURING NUMBERS OF PERSONNEL ACTIVATED AND DEPLOYED

We generate counts of activated reservists and deployed active-duty personnel from DMDC's Global War on Terrorism Contingency File. The Contingency File contains one record for each activation or deployment of a reserve or active-duty member in support of the Global War on Terrorism. Each record contains the beginning and end dates of the activation or deployment, the home address of the service member, and a county-level identifier for the unit from which the service member was activated or deployed. DMDC constructed this file from a variety of administrative data sources; the data are believed to be reasonably complete, although revisions to the file are ongoing.[14] Our extract of the Contingency File is dated December 2004.

We use the zip code of the reservist's home address and the zip code of the active-duty member's duty base to identify the member's county. If a zip code is not available, we then use the applicable county code. If neither is available, we drop the activation or deployment from our data. Missing zip and county codes cause us to drop about 2 percent of all reserve activations. We lose far more active-duty deployments (about 36 percent, overall) using this method.

The missing data are largely the result of active-duty deployments that originate from OCONUS bases (which do not have valid zip or county codes). This poses no problem for our analysis, provided that the active-duty personnel are in fact stationed abroad. In some cases, though, active-duty soldiers could be deployed from a duty unit formed for the purposes of deployment, and that duty unit could have been assigned a non-U.S. zip code (APO/FPO [Army/Fleet Post Office]), even though its members originated from bases located within the United

---

[14] End dates of activations and deployments are thought to be particularly prone to mis-measurement. Recorded end dates in some instances may be later than actual end dates. However, this particular problem is not thought to be widespread (author communication with Virginia Hyland, OSD-RA, November 18, 2004).

States.[15] With available data, we could not determine how common this phenomenon might be. We note here that active-duty personnel deployed from a ship are also dropped from our data, even if that ship is temporarily located in a harbor adjacent to a U.S. county. As described further below in this section, we implement our main regressions for employment at the county-month level, the lowest level of aggregation permitted by the QCEW and DMDC data. For reservists, we count the number of reservists serving on active duty in support of the Global War on Terrorism in each month according to the county of their recorded home address. For active-duty personnel, we count the number of active-duty personnel deployed in support of the Global War on Terrorism in each month according to the county of their duty unit. The county might be too fine a level of aggregation if, for example, activated reservists live in one county but are employed in a neighboring county or if, as is likely, the demand for goods and services encompasses several counties. Our main results were substantively unchanged when we implemented regressions at higher levels of aggregation. We report the Public Use Microdata Area (PUMA) and Super-PUMA level results in Appendix B.

ECONOMETRIC METHODS

Our basic regression specification models the determinants of total employment, N, in geographic area g (county) and period t (month) as

$$N_{gt} = R_{gt}\beta + A_{gt}\gamma + X_{gt}\theta + \mu_g + \tau_t + \varepsilon_{gt}, \qquad (3.1)$$

where R is reserve activations, A is active-duty deployments, and X is a vector of other control variables. This specification generalizes the specification in Equation 2.1. In addition to μ_g, a fixed effect to capture baseline employment in a geographic area g, it also includes a fixed effect, τ_t, for each time period (month). These time-level fixed effects capture national changes in employment from business cycle

---

[15] The fixed-effects specification we employ will be unaffected by this type of measurement error, provided that the measurement error is approximately constant within counties over the period of our data.

variations. We can think of Equation 3.1 as a difference-of-difference specification.[16] In addition, we include a regression residual, ε_{gt}.

To motivate the specification in Equation 3.1, note that the specification incorporates the polar supply-side hypotheses discussed in Section 2 ($\beta = -1$ / $\beta = 0$, $\gamma = 0$ / $\gamma = 1$). An alternative approach would specify the dependent variable in logs (i.e., log employment). However, adopting that approach leaves no such simple relationship between our null hypothesis and the econometric specification.

A second alternative would divide both the dependent and independent variables by an estimate of the county's population. The dependent variable would then be employment per capita, and the key independent variables would be activations or deployments per capita. However, when population is measured with error (as will almost always be the case), this specification will yield biased estimates of β and γ.[17]

The included county fixed effects, μ_{γ}, control for any county-level time-invariant factors. Our vector of other control variables, X, therefore needs only to include factors that vary within a county over time. Since our data cover only about four years, any such variable would need to vary at high frequency. We include the state unemployment rate, UR, and county population, P.[18]

Specifying the model in levels (i.e., the number of employees) rather than in logs (i.e., the logarithm of employees) raises its own specification issues. Counties vary widely in size. Los Angeles County, for example, has more than 5 million employees (out of 10 million people), but some counties across the country have fewer than 1,000 employees. This wide variation in the magnitude of the dependent variable is not an issue for independent variables also expressed in numbers of people (e.g., number of activated reservists, number of

---

[16] See, for example, Meyer (1995).

[17] This problem is known in the literature as "division bias." See, for example, Borjas (1980); Feldstein (1995); and Levitt (1998).

[18] We obtain estimates of the state unemployment rate from the BLS Local Area Unemployment Statistics program. The Census Bureau generates county population estimates as of July of each year. We use linear interpolation to obtain measures of population for the intervening months.

deployed active-duty personnel), but it is an issue for other variables, such as the unemployment rate and time-level fixed effects. It is not plausible that the unemployment rate or time trend has a constant effect on the number of employees, independent of the population of the county. On a priori grounds, a proportional effect seems more plausible. To address this issue, we enter the time-fixed effects and the unemployment rate in our regression in both levels and interacted with population:

$$N_{gt} = R_{gt}\beta + A_{gt}\gamma + P_{gt}\theta_1 + UR_{gt}\theta_2 + P_{gt}UR_{gt}\theta_3 +$$
$$\mu_g + \tau_t + P_{gt}\tau_t + \varepsilon_{gt} \qquad (3.2)$$

Thus, the specification in Equation 3.2 allows a one percentage point change in the state unemployment rate to cause a constant change in employment, a constant change in employment per capita (i.e., a proportional effect), or a linear combination of the constant and proportional effects. Similarly, the time effects are specified alone and interacted with county population. Again, this allows constant effects or effects proportional to population.

Consistent estimation of β and γ requires that variation in activations and deployment within counties is uncorrelated with factors that affect types of employment that are omitted from the model. This assumption seems plausible in this case, because the events of September 11, 2001, were clearly unexpected and because there is no evidence that DoD manages activations and deployments in any way that is related to local employment. For example, we have no reason to believe that DoD systematically activates reserve units from counties with downward-trending employment. It is possible, however, that reserve accessions are correlated with trends in employment, which could lead to a correlation between employment trends and activations.

Finally, we note that this is high-frequency data (monthly). Using monthly data allows us to capture the frequent changes in activations and precise timing of those activations. However, our use of high-frequency data raises two issues. First, firms might not respond immediately to the loss of an activated reservist. If a reservist works in part of the month in which he or she is activated, we would not see any effect of his or her activation until the following month. If it then takes another month for an employer to replace that reservist, then the gross effect of activation on employment might not be apparent until several months after the initial activation. We capture the possibility of such lagged effects by including not only the contemporaneous values for reserve activations and active-duty deployments but also values from earlier months (i.e., lagged values of the independent variable). Our estimation equation thus becomes

$$
N_{gt} = \sum_{l=0}^{L} R_{g,t-l}\beta_l + \sum_{m=0}^{M} A_{g,t-m}\gamma_m + P_{gt}\theta_1 + UR_{gt}\theta_2 + P_{gt}UR_{gt}\theta_3 + \mu_g + \tau_t + P_{gt}\tau_t + \varepsilon_{gt} \qquad (3.3)
$$

where L and M is the number of lags in reserve activations and active-duty deployments, respectively. We employ three lags in the regressions reported below.[19]

A second issue concerns the treatment of the residual in Equation 3.3, ε_{gt}. In time-series data, and especially in monthly time-series data, it is highly likely that the residual will be serially correlated because of slowly changing omitted variables. In general, the induced serial correlation leads to underestimation of the standard errors and, consequently, an increased likelihood of inferring statistically significant effects when no such inference is warranted. We account for serial correlation by computing standard errors assuming an AR(1) specification.[20]

SAMPLE SELECTION

We impose two restrictions on our database of county-level employment, activations, and deployments. First, we drop four counties that did not disclose total employment in our data. Second, we restrict our period of analysis to that time between January 2001 and December 2004. Our key explanatory variables—activations and deployments—are, by

---

[19] A likelihood ratio test suggested that models with three lags fit the data better than models with fewer lags. Adding a fourth lag provided little additional explanatory power. The gross effect of reserve activations and active-duty deployments was largely unaffected by the particular lag structure chosen.

[20] Our regressions are implemented in Stata v.8 using the xtregar procedure, which does not simultaneously account for heteroscedasticity. The reported estimated standard errors, therefore, might be biased downward in magnitude.

definition, zero between January and August of 2001, since the Global War on Terrorism begins officially on September 11, 2001. We include these earlier months with zero activations to provide a sufficiently long baseline from which we can reliably estimate county-level fixed effects.

Our final data set comprises 3,137 counties with observations over 47 months.[21] Table 3.1 presents the means and standard deviations of the regression variables for this final sample.

Table 3.1
Descriptive Statistics

	Mean	Standard Deviation
Monthly employment	40,293	143,655
Activated reserve personnel	31.5	95.6
Deployed active-duty personnel	20.4	376.2
Population	92,203	300,738
State unemployment rate	5.13	1.10
State unemployment rate × Population	5,013.2	17,878.9

---

[21] Our data actually span 51 months (October 2000–December 2004). In our regressions, however, we lose three months because of our lagged specification and lose one month because of the Cochrane-Orcutt transformation employed by the Stata procedure, xtregar.

4. ECONOMETRIC RESULTS

In this section, we present the results of estimating the econometric model of employment specified in Equation 3.3. We begin by presenting results for the entire sample. We then present results by county size, for fire and police employment only.[22]

OVERALL RESULTS FOR EMPLOYMENT

Our overall results with respect to employment indicate that employment declines in the first month of activation but then recovers over the subsequent three months. In column 1 of Table 4.1, the estimated coefficient on reserve activations in the current month is —1.164 (0.223), which is statistically significant at the 1 percent confidence level. The coefficient estimate implies that for every reservist activated in the current month, county employment declines by 1.4 workers. This estimate does not statistically differ from —1 and is consistent with the hypothesis that all reservists leave a civilian job when activated and that employers do not replace these activated reservists immediately. By itself, the coefficient estimate is also consistent with the hypothesis that reserve activations lower the demand for local goods and, therefore, depress local employment.

Column 2 of Table 4.1 adds lagged values of reserve activations and active-duty deployments to the specification. The coefficients on the lagged values of reserve activations suggest that employment begins to recover in subsequent months. The coefficient estimate on employment lagged one month is 0.708 (0.238), indicating that the total effect of reserve activations on county employment after two months is half as large as the contemporaneous effect (i.e., —0.705 vs. —1.413). Employment continues to recover in the second and third months following activation. The coefficient estimates on employment lagged two and three months are 0.282 (0.240) and 0.513 (0.235), respectively. Summing the impact of reserve activations on employment over the four months yields

---

[22] Appendix C shows results separately for the subperiods 2001–2002 and 2003–2004.

Table 4.1
The Effect of Activations and Deployments on Monthly Employment

	(1)	(2)
Activated reserve personnel		
t	−1.164	−1.413
	(0.223)***	(0.232)***
t − 1		0.708
		(0.238)***
t − 2		0.282
		(0.240)
t − 3		0.513
		(0.235)**
Deployed active-duty personnel		
t	0.090	0.092
	(0.025)***	(0.027)***
t − 1		0.018
		(0.028)
t − 2		−0.057
		(0.028)**
t − 3		0.053
		(0.027)*
Population	1.004	1.006
	(0.078)***	(0.078)***
State unemployment rate	−121.280	−121.487
	(9.924)***	(9.925)***
State unemployment rate × Population	−0.086	−0.086
	(0.004)***	(0.004)***
Constant	−5,445.018	−5,461.459
	(100.092)***	(99.989)***
n(total)[a]	147,439	147,439
n(counties)[b]	3,137	3,137
R^2	0.880	0.880
ρ	0.900	0.899
Gross activated[c]	—	0.090
		(0.367)
Gross deployed[d]	—	0.106**
		(0.041)

NOTES: Standard errors in parentheses. [a]Total number of county-year observations. [b]Total number of counties. [c]Sum of current and lagged coefficients on activated reserve personnel. [d]Sum of current and lagged coefficients on deployed active-duty personnel. *significant at 10%; **significant at 5%; ***significant at 1%.

an estimate of 0.09 (0.36), which is not statistically different from zero (see "gross activated" in Table 4.1, which sums coefficients on the current and lagged values of activated reserve personnel). Thus, although reserve activations have an immediate effect on local employment, four months later that effect has disappeared.

Our model estimates a small positive impact of active-duty deployments on local employment. In column 1 of Table 4.1, the coefficient estimate on active-duty deployments in the current month is a statistically significant 0.090 (0.025). The estimates of lagged effects are not precise, and no clear pattern exists. Nevertheless, the total effect of active-duty deployments after four months is about 0.11 (0.04) (see "gross deployed" in Table 4.1). This estimate suggests that a positive effect of active-duty deployments persists over time.

We interpret the regression results reported in Table 4.1 as evidence that employers cannot replace activated reservists in the very short term (i.e., within a few weeks of activation). This interpretation is consistent with a hiring process that takes time and a lack of advance warning to employers that a reservist is about to be activated. Within a few months, however, employers are able to find replacements for activated reservists, and so the gross impact of activations on employment declines to zero. Conversely, the regression results suggest that when activated reservists return home, employment initially increases as employers reemploy these activated reservists and then declines in the following months as temporary employees are laid off.

With respect to active-duty deployments, we interpret the results of Table 4.1 as evidence that local bases backfill some active-duty functions with civilian replacement workers, but at a ratio much less than one-for-one. Since active-duty soldiers are not counted in local employment data, the hiring of these civilian replacement workers causes local employment to rise. Another possibility is that the spouses of active-duty personnel enter the civilian labor market when their husbands or wives are deployed.

We acknowledge that other interpretations of these empirical findings are possible. As noted in Section 3, our econometric model estimates the correlation between equilibrium employment and activations and deployments and so cannot distinguish between supply- and demand-side explanations of why employment might respond to activations and deployments. We prefer the supply-side interpretation given above, but it is possible that activations and deployments affect local demand. In the case of reserve activations, for example, it is possible that employment declines in the short run because local demand for goods and services falls when reservists depart for active-duty service. It is unclear, however, why employment would then recover over the next few months. It is also unclear why changes in local demand would have such immediate effects on local employment given that hiring and firing employees are costly and often slow processes.

A demand-side explanation for our findings with respect to active-duty deployments might argue that the families of active-duty soldiers experience an increase in income from the receipt of deployment-related pays and that this increase in income raises the demand for local goods and, hence, local employment. If this were true, however, we would expect the impact of active-duty deployments on local employment to persist in the long run, a hypothesis that the results recorded in Table 4.1 do not support.

ANALYSES BY COUNTY SIZE

Much of the reporting on the impact of activations on local communities has focused on relatively small communities. It seems plausible that smaller local labor markets might make finding qualified temporary workers more difficult in smaller communities. As we showed in Section 2, smaller counties are also more likely to have a relatively high number of activated reservists, compounding the problem of finding replacement workers. To test this hypothesis, we divided our sample into four equally sized groups according to county population.[23] We report the results of these regressions in Table 4.2.

---

[23] The quartiles were defined as follows: 0—11,219; 11,220—25,060; 25,061—62,678; 62,679+.

Table 4.2
The Effect of Activations and Deployments on Monthly Employment,
by County Population Quartile

	County Population Quartile			
	1st	2nd	3rd	4th
Activated reserve personnel				
t	0.279	0.222	−0.485	−1.060
	(0.391)	(0.355)	(0.286)*	(0.479)**
t − 1	0.378	0.212	0.276	0.411
	(0.400)	(0.363)	(0.296)	(0.489)
t − 2	0.383	0.307	1.116	−0.071
	(0.404)	(0.367)	(0.299)***	(0.493)
t − 3	−0.137	−0.053	0.275	0.095
	(0.408)	(0.365)	(0.312)	(0.482)
Deployed active-duty personnel				
t	−0.062	−0.645	−0.005	0.095
	(0.161)	(0.201)***	(0.028)	(0.055)*
t − 1	−0.030	0.177	0.025	0.009
	(0.161)	(0.207)	(0.031)	(0.057)
t − 2	−0.049	−0.290	−0.017	−0.056
	(0.161)	(0.208)	(0.031)	(0.058)
t − 3	−0.061	0.135	−0.021	0.070
	(0.161)	(0.204)	(0.029)	(0.056)
Population	0.014	−0.722	0.180	1.029
	(0.357)	(0.327)**	(0.261)	(0.154)***
State unemployment rate	−22.484	37.932	36.179	−447.151
	(3.974)***	(16.128)**	(22.277)	(43.665)***
State unemployment rate × Population	−0.014	−0.547	−0.342	−0.058
	(0.057)	(0.090)***	(0.055)***	(0.009)***
Constant	1,098.015	1,989.949	3,333.289	−12,920.542
	(35.281)***	(80.517)***	(133.181)***	(655.806)***
n(total)[a]	36,848	36,848	36,848	36,895
n(counties)[b]	784	784	784	785
Gross activated[c]	0.903	0.688	1.182	−0.625
	(0.594)	(0.514)	(0.442)	(0.762)
Gross deployed[d]	−0.202	−0.623	−0.018	0.118
	(0.295)	(0.306)	(0.037)	(0.085)

NOTES: Standard errors in parentheses. [a]Total number of county-year observations. [b]Total number of counties. [c]Sum of current and lagged coefficients on activated reserve personnel. [d]Sum of current and lagged coefficients on deployed active-duty personnel. *significant at 10%; **significant at 5%; ***significant at 1%.

The results in Table 4.2 are inconclusive with respect to this hypothesis. Overall, the results suggest that we do not have enough power to stratify on county size. Put simply, not enough variation exists to estimate effects within quartiles. The only statistically significant effect of reserve activations on employment is in the largest counties. Counties with populations in the bottom three quartiles of the population distribution appear to be unaffected by reserve activations. Active-duty deployments appear to have a relatively strong negative impact on employment in counties in the second quartile of the population distribution. In all other quartiles, the impact of active-duty deployments is statistically indistinguishable from zero.

ANALYSES FOR PUBLIC SAFETY EMPLOYEES

Given the concern over the impact of reserve activations on the provision of public safety services, we present results in Table 4.3 separately for police and fire employment. Few counties disclose employment at the industry level; therefore, we estimate these regressions using state-level data. However, even at the state level, nondisclosure causes us to drop a large number of observations in these regressions. Only 34 states disclose police and fire employment.

Looking first at the impact of activations on police employment, we see that the coefficient on reserve activations in the current month is —0.080 (0.035), which is significantly different from zero at the 5 percent confidence level. In contrast to the results of Table 4.1, it appears that the negative impact of activations on police employment worsens over time. The net effect of activations on police employment after four months is —0.245 (0.051). We do not have a compelling explanation for why the effect of reserve activations on police employment should become greater over time.

It is difficult to interpret the magnitude of this coefficient. Even according to our strong null hypothesis (i.e., everyone working before activation and no replacement), we would not expect a decline of one police officer employed for every activation. The 2000 Reserve Component Survey suggests that about 5 percent (one in 20) of working reservists is working for a police department. If reserve activations were proportional to the occupation distribution, then we might divide the coefficients by 0.05 (i.e., multiply by 20). Doing so implies an adjusted coefficient of 4.9 (i.e., police employment declines by 4.9 for every activated reservist whose civilian job is in a police department). This effect seems implausibly large. It is quite possible, though, that this scaling factor is inappropriate for the states in our sample. In particular, perhaps police officers were more likely to be activated than other reservists were. This is possible for some periods of our data in which military police (MP) units were in high demand (assuming that MPs are more likely than non-MPs to be civilian police officers). Our estimates imply that reserve activations have no impact on employment in fire departments.

Table 4.3
The Effect of Activations and Deployments on Monthly Police and
Fire Employment

	Police		Fire	
	(1)	(2)	(3)	(4)
Activated reserve personnel				
t	−0.080	−0.060	0.006	0.011
	(0.035)**	(0.036)*	(0.023)	(0.024)
t − 1		−0.039		−0.018
		(0.031)		(0.021)
t − 2		−0.159		−0.007
		(0.030)***		(0.022)
t − 3		0.013		0.013
		(0.028)		(0.019)
Deployed active-duty personnel				
t	−0.009	−0.001	0.001	0.000
	(0.008)	(0.010)	(0.009)	(0.009)
t − 1		−0.007		0.000
		(0.010)		(0.011)
t − 2		−0.021		−0.001
		(0.009)**		(0.012)
t − 3		0.015		0.000
		(0.008)*		(0.011)
Population	−0.028	−0.029	−0.002	−0.001
	(0.017)*	(0.016)*	(0.008)	(0.008)
State unemployment rate	−70.214	−70.749	8.730	9.269
	(34.112)**	(33.603)**	(23.664)	(23.726)
State unemployment rate × Population	0.002	0.002	−0.000	−0.000
	(0.001)***	(0.000)***	(0.000)	(0.000)
Constant	−13,934	−8,867	−5,210	−5,206
	(959)***	(927)***	(55)***	(55)***
n(total)[a]	1,256	1,256	1,134	1,134
n(counties)[b]	34	34	32	32
Gross activated[c]	—	−0.245	—	−0.001
		(0.051)***		(0.033)
Gross deployed[d]	—	−0.001	—	−0.001
		(0.013)		(0.012)

NOTES: Standard errors in parentheses. [a]Total number of county-year observations. [b]Total number of counties. [c]Sum of current and lagged coefficients on activated reserve personnel. [d]Sum of current and lagged coefficients on deployed active-duty personnel. *significant at 10%; **significant at 5%; ***significant at 1%.

5. CONCLUSIONS

This report has presented results of an analysis of the impact of reserve activations and active-duty deployments on county-level employment. We conclude from this analysis that both the national and local impact of activations and deployments on employment is likely to be very small. Nationally, reserve activations in 2004 represented an average of only 0.13 percent of total employment; thus, reserve activations during the Global War on Terrorism, even though high by historical standards, are unlikely to have much of an effect on U.S. employment. At the employer level, our estimates suggest that employers do not replace activated reservists immediately, but do find replacement workers within several months of an activation. Our regression evidence further suggests that local civilian employment increases when active-duty personnel are deployed. This finding could be attributable to the use of civilian workers to backfill key active-duty functions and spouses of active-duty personnel entering the civilian labor market while their husbands or wives are deployed. Our empirical results are also consistent with activations and deployments leading to changes in the demand for local goods and services, but for the reasons outlined in Section 4, we prefer the supply-side interpretation given here.

We acknowledge, though, that some communities and some employers are likely to suffer when local reservists are activated. We provide some suggestive evidence that police departments might find it particularly difficult to replace activated reservists in the short run and that this could be particularly true in smaller communities. DoD's policy of exempting reservists from active-duty service whose absence could adversely affect national security (broadly construed) is sensible in this regard.

Future research on this topic might pay special attention to the impact of activations on smaller firms and the self-employed, neither of which could be examined with these data. The self-employed might be examined most fruitfully at the individual level, since individual earnings are most likely to be the best barometer of the financial well-being of self-employed individuals. Although the following claim needs to be empirically validated, we note that standard economic arguments would argue against finding substantial negative impacts of activations on the income of self-employed reservists. These self-employed reservists presumably chose reserve service because they thought it would, on net, benefit them. Consequently, we would not expect individuals who stand to lose their businesses if called to active duty to put themselves at risk of activation. In ongoing work, we find that the self-employed, on average, experience large earnings gains when activated; what happens to their earnings when they return from active duty is unknown at this time.

Similar reasoning might also apply to very small firms. While overt discrimination against reservists in hiring decisions is illegal, it seems entirely possible that employers could know whether a given applicant is a member of the Reserves and find legitimate reasons not to hire that individual if it seems too risky to do so. That is, we would not expect smaller employers to take large risks in hiring reservists who might one day be activated if those employers are not compelled or do not find it optimal to do so.

Finally, we note that the deployment of large numbers of National Guardsmen could have implications for the provision of homeland security. In addition to their role in national defense, the state National Guards are used for a variety of civilian purposes, the most prominent of which is disaster relief (e.g., forest fires, tornados, hurricanes, earthquakes, acts of terrorism). Nearly a decade ago, Brown et al. (1997) provided some discussion of this issue. More recently, DoD has assured state governors that at least 50 percent of their National Guard troops will be available to them at any given time,[24] but whether this policy appropriately balances the use of the National Guard between

---

[24] See, for example, remarks by National Guard spokesman Major John Toniolli quoted in Janofsky and Nagourney (2005).

domestic and foreign objectives is unclear and deserving of further research.

APPENDIX A. RESULTS FOR QUARTERLY EARNINGS

We implemented a regression model identical in all respects to that specified in Equation 3.3, but in which the dependent variable is quarterly earnings. Quarterly earnings are recorded in the Quarterly Census of Employment and Wages at the same level of geographic detail as is employment. In most states, earnings include gross wages and salaries, bonuses, stock options, tips and other gratuities, and the value of meals and lodging. Some states also include in total earnings employer contributions to deferred compensation plans, such as 401(k) plans. We express wages in constant 2004 dollars using the Consumer Price Index—Urban.

We note that quarterly earnings is the product of employment and earnings per employee and that activations and deployments can affect either term of this product. That is, activations and deployments can affect employment, for the reasons argued in Section 3, but might also affect average earnings. Average earnings could rise, for example, if the supply of labor is less than perfectly elastic at the prevailing wage or if activations and deployments increase the local demand for labor.

Table A.1 presents the results of these regressions. The estimates are less precisely estimated than the employment estimates, perhaps because the frequency of our wage observations leaves us with fewer observations and less variation in our data. The coefficient estimate on reserve activations in the current month is $710 ($19,399), which is not statistically different from zero. We note that it is the opposite sign from the employment regressions. The coefficient estimate on current active-duty deployments is $7,504 ($2,385). This coefficient has the same sign as in the employment regressions. However, this coefficient seems implausibly large. If employment increases by about one-tenth of one worker in the quarter for each deployed active-duty soldier (the estimated 0.11 from Table 4.1), then the wage estimate suggests that the marginally affected worker is earning more than $75,000 per quarter, which is implausibly large.

The implausibly large coefficient on active-duty deployments from this model causes us to question the validity of the earnings results. Note that the estimated coefficient on population in these models is about $165,000, which makes little sense and could be attributable to the difficulty of estimating an AR(1) model on a relatively short panel (due to the fact the earnings data are quarterly, not monthly). We note that we obtain much more sensible estimates of the impact of population on quarterly earnings in a fixed-effect model in which we do not allow for autocorrelated disturbances (the coefficient on population in these models is about $5,800—see column 3 in Table A.1). The estimated coefficient on reserve activations and active-duty deployments in these simple fixed-effect models is implausibly large, however.

Table A.1
The Effect of Activations and Deployments on Quarterly Earnings ($2004)

	(1)	(2)	(3)
Activated reserve personnel			
t	710	−155,140	121,867
	(19,399)	(29,907)***	(20,004)***
t − 1		197,592	
		(29,760)***	
Deployed active-duty personnel			
t	7,504	6,502	5,622
	(2,385)***	(3,284)**	(2,546)**
t − 1		3,383	
		(3,318)	
Population	165,277	164,263	5,780
	(23,911)***	(23,892)***	(176)***
State unemployment rate	−3,099,929	−3,306,687	−1,334,003
	(1,292,916)**	(1,292,657)**	(1,414,498)
State unemployment rate × Population	5,338	5,500	1,536
	(522)***	(522)***	(585)***
Constant	−37,268,079	−22,747,213	−129,800,909
			(17,413,942)***
	(17,705,310)**	(17,324,815)	
n(total)[a]	47,055	47,055	50,192
n(counties)[b]	3,137	3,137	3,137
Gross activated[c]	—	42,452	—
		(20,804)**	
Gross deployed[d]	—	9,884	—
		(2,618)***	

NOTES: Columns 1 and 2 are estimated via fixed effects with AR(1) disturbances. Column 3 is estimated via fixed effects. Standard errors in parentheses. [a]Total number of county-quarter observations. [b]Total number of counties. [c]Sum of current and lagged coefficients on activated reserve personnel. [d]Sum of current and lagged coefficients on deployed active-duty personnel. *significant at 10%; **significant at 5%; ***significant at 1%.

APPENDIX B. PUBLIC USE MICRODATA AREA (PUMA)—LEVEL RESULTS

Table B.1
The Effect of Activations and Deployments on Monthly Employment
Aggregated to PUMA and Super-PUMA Levels

	Super PUMA		PUMA	
	(1)	(2)	(3)	(4)
Activated reserve personnel				
t	−0.678	−0.835	−0.737	−0.880
	(0.507)	(0.524)	(0.370)**	(0.384)**
t − 1		0.449		0.558
		(0.536)		(0.393)
t − 2		0.299		0.112
		(0.540)		(0.396)
t − 3		0.353		0.117
		(0.534)		(0.390)
Deployed active-duty personnel				
t	0.074	0.084	0.093	0.094
	(0.077)	(0.082)	(0.045)**	(0.048)**
t − 1		−0.016		0.012
		(0.086)		(0.051)
t − 2		−0.034		−0.052
		(0.086)		(0.051)
t − 3		0.071		0.052
		(0.083)		(0.049)
Population	1.153	1.151	0.986	0.988
	(0.218)***	(0.218)***	(0.137)***	(0.137)***
State unemployment rate	−1,607.904	−1,610.296	−454.254	−454.871
	(141.556)***	(141.624)***	(35.842)***	(35.851)***
State unemployment rate × Population	−0.000	−0.000	−0.001	−0.001
	(0.000)	(0.000)	(0.000)***	(0.000)***
Constant	−35,673.502	−35,701.633	−13,813.615	−13,880.035
	(2,212.168)***	(2,209.905)***	(540.281)***	(540.051)***
n(Total)	18,988	18,988	48,175	48,175
n(PUMA)	404	404	1,025	1,025
Gross activated[a]	—	0.266	—	−0.093
		(0.843)		(0.616)
Gross deployed[b]	—	0.104	—	0.106
		(0.124)		(0.074)

NOTES: Standard errors in parentheses. [a]Sum of current and lagged coefficients on activated reserve personnel. [b]Sum of current and lagged coefficients on deployed active-duty personnel. *significant at 10%; **significant at 5%; ***significant at 1%.

APPENDIX C. EMPLOYMENT RESULTS BY SUBPERIOD

Our sample spans two distinct phases of the Global War on Terrorism: (1) the immediate aftermath of September 11, 2001, and the war in Afghanistan and (2) the invasion of Iraq and continued post-invasion operations in that country. The nature of deployments during those two periods differ in many ways, but perhaps most importantly by the sheer number of deployed personnel and the length of those deployments. It is conceivable that employer expectations about deployments changed over this period and that employers adjust differently to shorter expected absences of their reserve employees than they do to longer expected absences. Thus, it is possible that our estimated coefficients on reserve activations and active-duty deployments will change across the years in our data. To test this hypothesis, we implement our employment regressions separately for the periods 2001–2002 and 2003–2004. We report the results of these regressions in Table C.1.

Table C.1 The Effect of Activations and Deployments on Monthly Employment: 2001–2002 vs. 2003–2004

| | 2001–2002 | | 2003–3004 | |
	(1)	(2)	(3)	(4)
Activated reserve personnel				
t	−0.888	−0.968	−2.671	−2.819
	(0.463)*	(0.485)**	(0.247)***	(0.269)***
t − 1		−2.191		0.744
		(0.510)***		(0.278)***
t − 2		3.424		−0.625
		(0.524)***		(0.278)**
t − 3		0.483		0.427
		(0.530)		(0.266)
Deployed active-duty personnel				
t	0.409	0.239	0.012	0.022
	(0.134)***	(0.141)*	(0.026)	(0.028)
t − 1		0.247		0.001
		(0.150)*		(0.030)
t − 2		0.660		−0.063
		(0.165)***		(0.030)**
t − 3		−0.200		0.054
		(0.165)		(0.028)*
Population	2.039	2.023	1.975	1.983
	(0.123)***	(0.123)***	(0.119)***	(0.119)***
State unemployment rate	−101.573	−101.736	−140.491	−141.085
	(14.715)***	(14.710)***	(13.966)***	(13.966)***
State unemployment rate × Population	−0.122	−0.120	−0.072	−0.071
	(0.007)***	(0.007)***	(0.006)***	(0.006)***
Constant	−21,207.038	−20,608.011	−9,451.511	−9,577.972
	(308.723)***	(309.420)***	(264.242)***	(265.805)***
N(total)[a]	72,151	72,151	72,151	72,151
N(counties)[b]	3,137	3,137	3,137	3,137
Gross activated[c]		0.748		−2.272
		(0.752)		(0.366)
Gross deployed[d]		0.945		0.014
		(0.238)		(0.038)

NOTES: Standard errors in parentheses. [a]Total number of county-year observations. [b]Total number of counties. [c]Sum of current and lagged coefficients on activated reserve personnel. [d]Sum of current and lagged coefficients on deployed active-duty personnel. *significant at 10%; **significant at 5%; ***significant at 1%.

Over the 2001–2002 period, the coefficient estimates on reserve activations and active-duty deployments are comparable to those reported in Table 4.1, although the standard errors on those estimates are larger. Over the 2003–2004 period, the results suggest that reserve activations have a much stronger negative impact on county employment, and those effects do not dissipate with time (gross effect of −2.272).

Further analysis indicates that the 2003–2004 results are driven by the 2004 data. That is, we obtain results similar to those reported in Table 4.1 if we restrict the sample to 2001–2003. We explored whether outliers in the data in 2004 could explain the results, but we could not find a sample restriction that supported this hypothesis. Thus, we are uncertain how to interpret the 2003–2004 results. It could be that employers behaved quite differently in 2004 than they did in 2001–2003, or it could simply be that our fixed-effect AR(1) regression specification produces unreliable results in short panels.

REFERENCES

Bureau of Labor Statistics, *BLS Handbook of Methods*, U.S. Department of Labor, 1997. Available online at http://www.bls.gov/opub/hom/home.htm (as of November 2005).

——, "County Employment and Wages Technical Note," July 19, 2005. Available online at http://www.bls.gov/news.release/cewqtr.tn.htm (as of November 2005).

Borjas, George, "The Relationship Between Wages and Weekly Hours of Work: The Role of Division Bias," *Journal of Human Resources*, Vol. 15, No. 3, 1980, pp. 409–423.

Brown, Roger Allen, John Schank, Carl Dahlman, and Leslie Lewis, *Assessing the Potential for Using the Reserves in Operations Other Than War*, Santa Monica, Calif.: RAND Corporation, MR-796-OSD, 1997.

Clinton, Hillary Rodham, Remarks delivered at the "Transforming the Reserve Component for the 21st Century" conference, Washington, D.C., September 13, 2004.

Congressional Budget Office, *The Effects of Reserve Call-Ups on Civilian Employers*, May 2005.

Defense Manpower Data Center, Human Resources Strategic Assessment Program, *Reserve Component Members as First Responders/Emergency Services*, Survey Note No. 2005-001, Arlington, Va., 2005.

Defense Manpower Data Center, Survey and Program Evaluation Division, *May 2004 Status of Forces Survey of Reserve Component Members: Administration, Datasets, and Codebook*, DMDC Report No. 2004-013, Arlington, Va., 2004.

Doyle, Collin M., Glenn A. Gotz, Neil M. Singer, and Karen W. Tyson, *Analysis of Employer Costs from Reserve Component Mobilization*, Alexandria, Va.: Institute for Defense Analyses, 2004.

Feldstein, Martin, "College Scholarship Rules and Private Savings," *American Economic Review*, Vol. 85, No. 3, 1995, pp. 552–566.

Finer, Jonathan, "Iraq Is Affecting Small State in a Big Way: Vermont Has the Most Deaths Per Capita," *Washington Post*, February 9, 2005, p. A1.

Hooker, Mark A., and Michael M. Knetter, "Measuring the Economic Effects of Military Base Closures," Working Paper 6941, National Bureau of Economic Research, 1999.

Janofsky, Michael, and Adam Nagourney, "Governors Concerned Over National Guard Deployments in Iraq," *New York Times*, July 17, 2005.

Infield, Tom, "On the Home Front," *Philadelphia Inquirer*, August 1, 2005.

Klerman, Jacob A., David S. Loughran, and Craig Martin, *Early Results on Activations and the Earnings of Reservists*, Santa Monica, Calif.: RAND Corporation, TR-274-OSD, 2005.

Levitt, Steven D., "Why Do Increased Arrest Rates Appear to Reduce Crime: Deterrence, Incapacitation, or Measurement Error?" *Economic Inquiry*, Vol. 36, No. 3, 1998, pp. 353—372.

Mehren, Elizabeth, "A Town Called to Duty: For a Rural Vermont Community, the Conflict in Iraq Hits Home; With Its Guardsmen Deployed, Locals Band Together to Cover Their Absence," *Los Angeles Times*, May 2, 2005.

Meyer, Bruce, "Natural and Quasi-Experiments in Economics," *Journal of Business and Economic Statistics*, Vol. 13, No. 2, 1995, pp. 151—161.

Poppert, Patrick E., and Henry W. Herzog, Jr., "Force Reduction, Base Closure, and the Indirect Effect of Military Installations on Local Employment Growth," *Journal of Regional Science*, Vol. 43, No. 3, 2003, pp. 459—481.